FINDING STUFF

DAVID C. MILLER

Copyright©2018 David C. Miller
All Rights Reserved
Published by Unsolicited Press

No part of this book may be reproduced or transmitted in any form or by any means without written permission from the publisher or author.

Printed in the United States of America.

Attention schools and businesses: for discounted copies on large orders, please contact the publisher directly.

ISBN: 978-1-947021-51-8

Lovera Wolf Miller,
the purpose of every poem
and
Sasha, Brienna, Kash, Wyatt, & Ryka Jane

Poems

Dogwood	8
Death Defining Acts	9
Redbud	10
Verse 76	11
The war of words sonnet	12
marriage verse	13
19	14
a good poem	15
A non-mathematical lyrical expression of: $E_{in} - E_{out} = Q - W$ (Conservation of Energy)	16
A single long shadow	17
about poems and poets	18
analysis	19
face value	20
Finding Stuff	21
Fruit-cup	22
I like poems	23
I walked through the sky	24
MY epic poem	25
Lacunar Love	26
Leisure suit	27
She loves to fly	28
poetics	29
Swimmers	30
The Craftsman	31
Home and Garden	32
[Haiku by the numbers]	33
Calamitous Climatologist	34
dead reckoning	35
in the manner of an elegy	36
in other words	37
Funeral	38
lyric worry	39
Reader *(another word for critic)*	40
She asked	41
The Assayer	42

The composition	43
When I was Tommy,	44
a you love me love poem	46
About the Author	47
About The Press	48

FINDING STUFF

Dogwood

Incandescent dogwood blossoms brighten as the evening fades,
Heralding the final moments of short-lived spring.
Amelanchiers had their day, as did teaser tulips,
      long on bud—short on display.
Crab apples burst and showered petals in the briefest hour.

Only dogwood's white abides,
As both the crest and the tide,
      the body and the tail,
      the gasp,
           and the wail...

The end of spring is a metaphorical thing, beauty fading not yet
      decaying,
At worst a superficial sadness, looming a long summer of greening
      grasses,
Like lovers parting,
      with a long and tender embrace,
           dogwoods, leafing—

I keep thinking—
      it's the flowers,
      it's the flowers,
      it's the flowers!
I keep hoping spring is the thing,
while all the star-crossed seasons scream fall, fall, fall.

Death Defining Acts

tips of the maple tree limbs are on fire
only this morning were luminous green
I hear their mournful combustion of time
paled exhaled in the heartbreak blue sky
the sparrows have all flocked and fled
wan lingering flowers lean low
      the red ones
      are the black-flat dead ones
the tawny coats of the white-tailed deer
turn chestnut, turn coffee, turn grey
there is hardly a moment left of light!
it is night—
      that defines the day.

Redbud

a redbud blossoms by the side of the road
reaching out from under a sycamore
cautious tender and full of light
her panting pulses breathing bright
the supple roots aching deep
awakened from their frozen sleep
in haste to be the forest first
to sing with sun and quench her thirst
but first to blossom first to fade
her innocence and hope betrayed
overwhelmed by nature's green
of denser dreams and unforeseen

the heart's winter remembers well
where in thoughts only does beauty dwell

Verse 76

    ,written backward were words the all If
    right margin biased the Against
    ,still rise sun sacred the not Would
    ?night from day the joy with Refresh
    ,undo spring boundless the not Would
    ?winter formless stark-cold The
    ,unite muse the of music Does
    ?banter voguish in sing merely Or

Old words swathe lovely with true,
There is only beauty, love, and you!

The war of words sonnet

Reading a poem resurrects past masters,
The battle sounds of disembodied verse.
It's not the meanings that causes disasters,
But in formation lurks a hard-formal curse.

Conscripted writers rebuff the old form,
And order their words on the page.
Deserters strip-off their torn uniforms,
Bare-fisted, bare-chested, bare-righteous with rage.

Pain weeps from pages and aims the rifle,
With quatrains a holster and couplets the gun.
Oh God have mercy the sound is so awful.
Quick crack and flame the front-line's undone.

Dead masters encrypted a harsh-code upon it,
This soldier bleeds words to compose a damned sonnet.

marriage verse

his words were contradictions
of his other words
and his lines belied intentions
of anarchy, disunity, and despair
she seemed at first defenseless
except her form was effortless
and brilliant, and lovingly fair
together their life a poem
his rebellious impulse
her aesthetic calm
an entente cordiale that seemed to work,
               sometimes
      better tha
             n oth
                   ers

19

The first time I read it, March air was crisp
and all things unaligned, at nineteen
a grey day filled with papers and slips
a cloistered cog in the learning machine
When Hopkins shook foil the world flashed a beauty
I had neither imagined nor dreamed
the stanzas were surf songs singing on sand
for one who had never seen sea
clear violet blue-burning bright over land
breathing, breathing words into reality

a good poem

it flows like a river and expands aqua
like a sea
and when you jump in
the cold refreshness
quickly gives way to a searing salt
up your nose
and, and a damn burning
in your eyes
it pours through you
like zero-degree gin
waving hello to your bleeding folly
all the while drawing you up
in foam
then crashes you headlong
onto the beach
and while still stunned it calmly withdraws
and, and pounds you back again, again
every time you read it

A non-mathematical lyrical expression of: $E_{in} - E_{out} = Q - W$ (Conservation of Energy)

the scandalous thing
about a poem that sings...
is the way that it sounds
when you're not around!

A single long shadow

a single long shadow, reminder of his defiant quiet
and a face like stubbled November cornfields
it's all that remains— a few lines of verse
and some letters...
one woman claimed she'd miss him,
the one
who left empty lipstick-rimmed cognac glasses
on the night stand, and never cleaned a skillet,
not once
did they acknowledge their approaching separation
the hope of heaven looked Kandinsky
rancio, heady, unearthly, unspeakable
during daytime they thought together
but at night, they dreamed apart
their children radiated in another universe
as his contracted into particles and waves
and self-censored darkness.

gravity of tone, the final threadbare force
has, in the end,
limits—
beyond which even words lose their attraction
stretched letters scatter into scribble
ink evaporates, the dent of its imprint
flattens into the final illiterate horizon
"Hold on, hold on," she said,
"I'm coming, to read for you."

about poems and poets

a poem is a road
and words are its stone surface
pebbled, cobbled, bolder blocked, or paved
its blue lines intersecting red lines and black dots
across an unfolding imaginary map

poets are gemologists
(some precious stones strategically strewn)
they usually work from the conventional quarry
limestone usually will do
and freed from the constraint of destination, directions hardly
        matter—

Whitman constructed rambling rough thoroughfares
Williams only short narrow paths
Bishop fingered the edges of every rock before paving
Plath rolled the pavement smooth with her belly and her back
Eliot looked at paving stones, and imagined a cathedral
Stevens looked at the stones and imagined miniature sculptures
        within
Frost took an axe and first cleared the trees
Carroll anticipated the road ahead and walked backward
Pound sifted through the entire pile, choosing only righteous rock
Dickinson's lanes were covered with diamonds
Hopkins' boulevards glowed and inclined
Yeats' aggregate country lanes curved gloriously
Heaney laid straight blacktop

and I am an ordinary road worker
        grinding gravel, dreaming concrete

analysis

at first look it was clear, she was different
a noble brow, an epic chin, and in between
a hazelnut eye surprise
eyes that looked back into mine
I could have walked away, but couldn't

her body possessed her form
(and to this day I can barely explain)
like heat within the smoke
quivering above embers
of what, at one time, grew wild in the woods

imagine my surprise
when I removed, at last, her sweater,
she graciously yielded her blouse
and struggling with the catch, in time
the skirt too fell away

all those happy days (and nights), confessed, content
did she press upon me the beauty of her soul?
no, I took what I could,
and loved her like a poem
I loved her then, and still

face value

if you'd please step back a little, sir
you'll see,
she's perfect—
put together quite exquisitely.
with an engaging bounce in her step—
coming and going.
it little matters
which products were consumed,
in the styling of her hair,
or the pedigree of her pretty,
lilac underwear.
try to unwrap her, sir, if you will
and risk her unabridged
scorned smack slap against your skill.
the greedy pleasures of the heart
notwithstanding
would you abuse a single word
to critique a p a r t
any note of Herren Mozart?

Finding Stuff

"Mom, I'm going to freeze, I've lost my keys!"
So begins her magic, proceeding in reverse.
My wife can find the smallest thing, a hundred miles away.
She believes it's logic, but I know otherwise.
Her inner-mom-eye opens, the thing itself responds.
Joining in a nether land, the longing of the lost unfound.
She should write the poems.

Fruit-cup

My mother was a Braeburn apple,
tart, firm, and held up well to baking.

My sister, was a Seckel pear,
soft, oh so sweet, and too tender to keep.

They lie side by side now, on the back side,
of Pine Lake Cemetery.

I like to think,
They're holding hands in the loam beneath the frost,
whispering fruit-cup recipes.
It's been 10 years mother, 40 sister—

The Chapel of Peace,
must be on the other side,
nearer the lake.

1 like poems

that are short
and fit nicely
on one page
I usually know a good one
when I see one
and it matters to me
how the lines form a certain shape
how the form undulates
and
I hate rhymes
they really give me a headache.

that's all I have to say,
about poems I like;
    that's it,   oh:
and I lose—
       interest if they keep repeating, Repeating.... with pointy-
headed punctuation; and,
Nothing.
                      New to say, or when
    they lose their form or visual
                              appeal

Like this one.

I walked through the sky

I walked through the sky, not knowing the way.
A crow asked me why, why I wandered all day

My impulse to think, made him pivot and say,
"I'll try not to wink, if you'll try not to pray."

I stumbled and fell, through the carpet of cloud.
He cawed his farewell, "Have faith in the crowd."

There is no tomorrow, apart from today.
There's plenty of sorrow, and I'm on my way.

Through white then black I fell further still.
I questioned the pact, and dark dreadful thrill.

Falling's not freedom, there's just one way to go.
I'll splat in a kingdom, of damned vertigo.

I scan for a net, a safe place to land.
Rope, chopper, or jet, look! she's extending her hand.

I grab her so tightly, I think she might break.
I pray for her nightly, my soul she might forgive, I mean, take.

MY epic poem

It was a mighty pile
Of words like a giant wave,
Moving impossibly slowly, but possibly rising, above
The kelp like a leisurely earthquake.
Stalling on a reef of dissimilar similes, abject adverbs, and grinding
Sand in my mouth like I should have a drink,
Or something.

Then it curled back, if you can believe it, stretching
My patience like a wet cat
Waiting for a blow-dry.
If not for the unusual green in the blue, I
Would have deleted the page.
Not content with asphyxiation, the deconstructing dramatic arch
Paused
Before the parched beach,
And without comparison ended
Flat like a tilting horizon of dissolving concrete,
Like
If you waded in too deep
It would suck
The boots right off your soul.

Lacunar Love

he saw clouds among the faces
and brush strokes at despair
some type of reverse imagination
something broken, in need of repair

he watched unmoved a scene play out
there was a hand upon her thigh
imagine his surprise to learn
it was his hand, and it was her sigh

he never knew there was enough
until he had too much, so
she shouldn't expect him to know what's missing
unless he'd seen the whole

he saw it in her tender eyes
he couldn't quite hold in gaze
like a flower growing in a poem
missing petals, of an unturned phrase

she kept believing his heart was good
in spite of all the blood
the gaping hole explained it all
and she died, from his lacunar love

Leisure suit

polyester nearly bankrupt Nicaragua, who knew
a leisure suit's sour and salacious slice
could bludgeon bolls of white blood
from across a sea
of idling barges knocking timbers in Memphis
the old kings divested, diversified, deflected
but nothing suited the fallow fields
and while the gins rusted, the busted workers
got ginned, lost their grins, moved north
and wore wool
meanwhile cotton-less fashion
convulsed the couture
mercifully, most of the photos have been burned

She loves to fly

Longitude intersects longing somewhere north of sixty,
Otherwise we'd be regents of the sultry southern skies.
Vagabondage notwithstanding, a dusty case is not worth having.
Eccentricities power our electric kinetic bearing-bent routes.
Radial trajectory like desperate fledglings flung from the nest.
Abetments prompt daring, we sing steering at the wing!
Motion potion trip-buzz lotion sooths our vagrant sky dive lives.

poetics

what we need is some rhy-thm and some mo-tion
some rhy-thm and mo-tion
rhy-thm an' mo-tion
rhy-thm n' mo-tion
rhy-thm n mo-tion
rhy-thm n mo— clink.
need some rhy-thm and mo-tion— clutch,
we need rhy-thm and mo-tion— engage...
rhy-thm and mo-tion
rhy-thm n mo-tion
(ahhh)
rhy-thm n motion
(ohhh)
rhyth-mo, rhyth-mo, rhyth-mo,
rhytn—clink.
Shit

ryth-clink, ryhty-clink,
rtck%mt#-, - .

oh, fu#k it

Swimmers

we sleep like synchronized swimmers
arm over arm we stroke like one
side by side through the eider down seas
immersed in years of practice
alternating kicks, backstrokes, crawls
gliding, cresting, breathing—
in the deepest dark-waters
we fathomed buddy-breathing,
surfaced, and survived.
together we crossed channels, oceans
cold-tossed salty surf and warm sheet-still shallows.
swam up-stream, it seemed, for years
too stubborn to stop or, more likely, afraid
the other might drown.

beside you, every awakening a revelation
your body—next to mine—
with the leanness and economy
of intended travel
shivering
glistening

The Craftsman

The Craftsman 12" circular shrieks,
with what sounds like pleasure.
Yellow pine No. 2 rolls over, plays possum,
its insides spewing the finality of its fragrance—

This is harder than it smells.
The past has taught me; wear sturdy gloves,
protect the eyes—
In spite of all that, the aching hammers.
It must, it must be worked upon,
and at some point, they say, completed.

Ideally, late night quiet, extravagant time,
measuring twice, and twice-twice more.
Absolute parallels are hard to hear,
Star stillness winks, and, I think,
almost admires the clamor.

I break for sunrise, stretch, pour coffee,
and imagine the appraisal.
The realtor says enough with all these words.
I wonder if dreaming gets us farther,
or closer,
to it.

Home and Garden

Maple leaves shine shimmering in a sun splashed spring,
The wood's air breathes again, it's warm moist earth-breath sigh.
Field mice chip at their little chippy chores,
And tender tossed skies go a-streaming by.

Puzzled painted butterflies pause among the rushes,
Sniff the scents of purple petals basking in the day.
Chatty sounds of robins chirping rustle from the bushes,
And all the world's a happy place when every day is May.

Children's voices carry bright out across the grasses,
Echo back against the porch and then on down the road.
The sun it seems to shine forever whiter than before,
And peaceful smiling flies the flies, and jumps the happy toad.

"But this ain't all there is." Claims the buzzy bumbling bee.
"I've got a screaming stinger tucked up underneath my wings,
And I have seen the blue skies black at night and in the storm."
Maybe May is music still but oh, she's darker songs to sing.

"Forget all that." says the cat, stretched out upon the clover.
"This garden's fine, it's apple time, when juicy mice are grown."
We shan't pretend now at the end, that all's a merry rainbow,
But know our place, and hold our own, and love our garden home.

[Haiku by the numbers]

One: winter alone
Two: warm earth grows cherry trees
Mad mystery: three

Calamitous Climatologist

Thunderous sunshine,
struck the region unexpectedly,
    overnight.
We sent out the satellite trucks,
but lost them in the unseasonable fog.
We half-expected,
this front to move there,
or perhaps over there.
I guess the computer modeling...
Anyway,
tomorrow looks pretty much like yesterday,
but since we got that wrong, who knows.
The current weather pattern,
is reminiscent of what was seen in '75,
when my wife consented to marriage.
Speculation about climate change is not new.
More on this at ten, or eleven, not really sure.
Apart from that,
We are predicting more,
forecastastrophies,
for the unforeseeable future.
This is your undermanned weatherman,
signing off, until I see you again—
perhaps yesterday.

dead reckoning

fountain grass caves at first frost
    mash-matted decay-drooped stalks
pale sky is emptied of song
    robins having plumped, are now gone
windows closed-shuttered are locked
    only silence from the unwinding clock
soul-savaged strangers compare
    dark-strangled empty
    despair
time augers fragments of season
    intent in razing what,
    reason?
death has a way of discerning
    which hope is the pivot for
    turning

in the manner of an elegy

mourning is like morning,
    wait, stop.
mourning is like pre-morning,
    no, that's weak.
mourning is a perverse parody of pre-morning,
    yeah, that's closer.

Mourning is an aubade made most bitter,
suspended stillness before the unlit light,
but there's no light,
spent anticipation of a new day,
but there is not one.
It's stuck time,
weary time.
It's a stinking dead lark on the lawn,
where shadows cast darkness, and
all the words get strangled by a crowd,
of naked strangers.

My mother stirs her coffee,
clinking the spoon.
She never sips, and never looks up.
We sit at her kitchen table.
I guess we are waiting,
for the morning news to come on.

There's no news.

in other words

I want to read something,
that can't be paraphrased,
outlined, or
syllabolized. I want more—
one-shot noun-ish verbs,
coincidental rimes,
dismantled times, that are,
    intentionally un-tappable.
I want a verbatim moment
with,
a poet's singing snowflake soul.
I'm done with smart.

Funeral

Wyatt reaches from his fathers' arms—
leans down to kiss his great-grandfather,
one last time.
with thought as crystal as the sunburst morning,
(the way only a three-year-old can think)
his cheeks flush with revelation,
he looks back over his shoulder toward his mother, and with brows
in genuine furrow says,
"He's cold now."

lyric worry

She is worried,
about my worrying—
Like the other day at the concert,
when the wind picked-up,
a chorus of rabbits fell,
out of the tree,
right onto the loud speakers.
My goal is forgetting,
sounds like this— and other songs,
that cannot be unheard.
I struggle to forget what I never knew.
C'mon,   **bun** ny | **lyr** ics | **have** no | **tune**.
They're **mere** ly | **mu** si cal | **met** a phors.
It's easier to just remember...

You see, that's why,
I am inclined to let her worry.

Reader
(another word for critic)

readers are sanctioned voyeurs
specializing in spectacled inspections
old metronome in one hand,
older thesaurus the other—
prying apart purposeful phrases
their peering hands smudging the glass
imagining how they would say
what I cannot say any other way—

if you could avert your eyes a moment,
please, while I put on my robe.

She asked

She asked,
if I'd please explain,
the difference between prose and poetry.
(We've been through this before.)
I once said it's the difference,
between evening and twilight.
"Humm," she said, "that doesn't help...
is it the new words, the lack of transition,
the absolute devotion to the left margin,
      the odd off-sets, a strain
      devoid of instruments,
the, how shall we say, intentional obscurity,
or the technical stuff?"
Good prose, I venture, is the fine-woven linen,
tablecloth of a feast,
covering the table's dimensions,
protecting the table from spilt gravy,
its crisp white contrasting the green and red salad.
Poetry is the inherited lace runner.
In its own way, it too covers the table,
(like a song that fills the room)
nothing is placed upon it
except, perhaps, a vase of fresh flowers.
It's the part of the meal,
that sates your soul.

The Assayer

This is madness. The Laws of Nature are more like optional ordinances,
of mathematics. Closets filled with gaffes, volumes of fine print—
disclaimers up the Yin Yang.
Galileo proved the tides
    proved, the earth
        proved its motion,
            proved the sun
                proved the center— ha!
Like many truths, error is somewhere in the layers,
of its Cronbach's alpha.
If he missed, somehow, something big
like the moon,
what else is missing?

Is truth simply the hidden trap door, under garbage can No. 814,
at the end of a menacing dark alley?
When there is no reasonable escape— there opens an imaginative one?
Does genius metaphor bend the beam of truth?

Tell me master, did you really think,
a crescent moon of Venus,
would convince the Pope?

The composition

This will not work, she said
Check your angle, she said
Look how the slant sun
Bends blue snow into gold—
Back-off your ef, she said
Open up, she said
If you listen to your internal
Conversation, you are doomed.
Nothing looks right, she said
Where is the focus, she said
The composition has no life
Until it breathes—
Take your foot off, she said
Off its neck, she said
So, my little flower, if I let you go
Will your petals fly to the horizon—
or expand into a blossom?

When I was Tommy,

I might have met the Acid Queen.
If only I had heard, the tympani!
Rolling, as it tends to do,
Across dark dreams,
Laying up upon my sternum,
Columns, cords, and cables.
I'm pretty sure, I felt her,
On my sternum or in.
Perhaps it was her "healing" hands,
Prying open my screamless mouth.
They say she meant well.

When I was a honey-smoked,
Turkey sandwich on wheat,
Strangers stared at me.
Trapped as I was
in a chilled display case
With my face pressed upon
The cellophane wrapper,
I imagined they imagined
me with mustard,
Or mayo, and salt.
I think I tried to scream, but
The vibration of the refrigeration,
Drowned me out.
Some vegetarians stared in disgust,
So I feigned soy-turkey,

When I was an asshole
Well, you can probably guess,
I stared into the empty bowl
And the expectations were
Overwhelming.

When I was dead,
(Isn't that the point of all this anyway?)

Things were looking up and
I saw, for the first time,
Real grassroots.

a you love me love poem

I love you like paths love boots
like harp strings love fingers
like spillage loves sponges

I love you like books love a reader
like sun love shade
like crystal loves cognac

I love you like rain loves dogwoods
like pizza loves hunger
like mowers love grass

I love you like songs love throats
like whispers love secrets
like April loves May

I love you like love poems love metaphors
but your love
loves me like no other

About the Author

Following a series of poor choices, David Miller eventually graduated with a degree in English from Purdue University. Subsequently, he made one mistake after another resulting in extended periods of study at the University of Iowa, Cal State Long Beach, the University of California at Riverside, and UCLA. All that changed when his muse consented to marriage. He showered, shaved and went to medical school at Loma Linda University, Loma Linda, California. He is in practice in Indiana, which is well situated for clandestine bohemian pursuits. He has authored twenty science-related articles, and was the co-author of a non-fiction book, (*Womenopause*, O-Books, London, UK, 2010). Recent poetry has appeared in *Metaphor, Harbinger Asylum, Deronda Review, Sacred Cow, Leaves of Ink, Haiku Journal, Ancient Paths Literary Journal, Dunes Review,* and *Canary.* Learn more at davidcmillerauthor.wordpress.com.

About The Press

Unsolicited Press is a small press in Portland, Oregon. The press was founded in 2012 by a group of editors and writers who were tired of watching big publishers ignore true literary work in exchange for commercial commodities. The team seeks to produce phenomenal, sometimes experimental, poetry, fiction, and creative nonfiction. Learn more at www.unsolicitedpress.com.

www.ingramcontent.com/pod-product-compliance
Lightning Source LLC
Chambersburg PA
CBHW071758080526
44588CB00013B/2290